# My Sight Word List



English

| | | |
|---|---|---|
| a | in | said |
| and | is | see |
| away | it | the |
| big | jump | three |
| blue | little | to |
| can | look | two |
| come | make | up |
| down | me | we |
| find | my | where |
| for | not | yellow |
| funny | one | you |
| go | day | |
| help | play | |
| here | red | |
| I | run | |

Name: _________________ Date: __________

Today is: Monday | Tuesday | Wednesday
Thursday | Friday

Direction: Trace and read the sentences.

| fun | gun | run | sun |

They are having fun.

He has a gun.

The bear is running.

The sun is smiling.

Name

### Draw a Picture

## I Can...

- [ ] use a Capital Letter
  <u>T</u>he cat is big.

- [ ] use spaces

- [ ] sound out words
  d-o-g = dog

- [ ] use a Period .

- [ ] Draw a picture

He is having fun, running under the sun with his new toy gun.

| fun  | gun 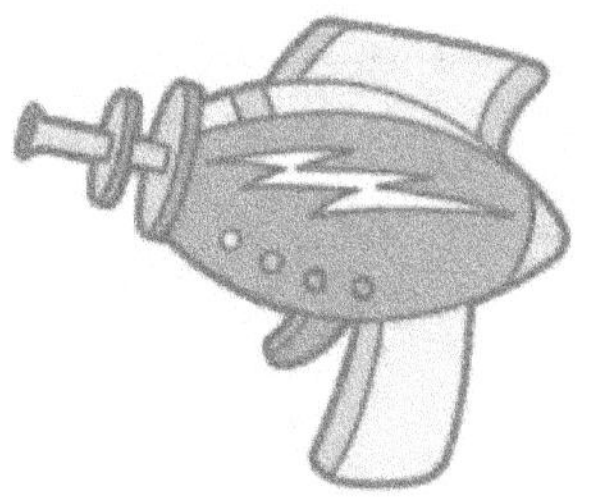 | run  | sun  |
|-----|-----|-----|-----|

Name: _________________ Date: _________

Today is: Monday | Tuesday | Wednesday | Thursday | Friday

Direction: Trace and read the sentences.

| **bag** | **rag** | **tag** | **wag** |

He has many bags.

I see a rag.

I see a tag.

Its tail is wagging.

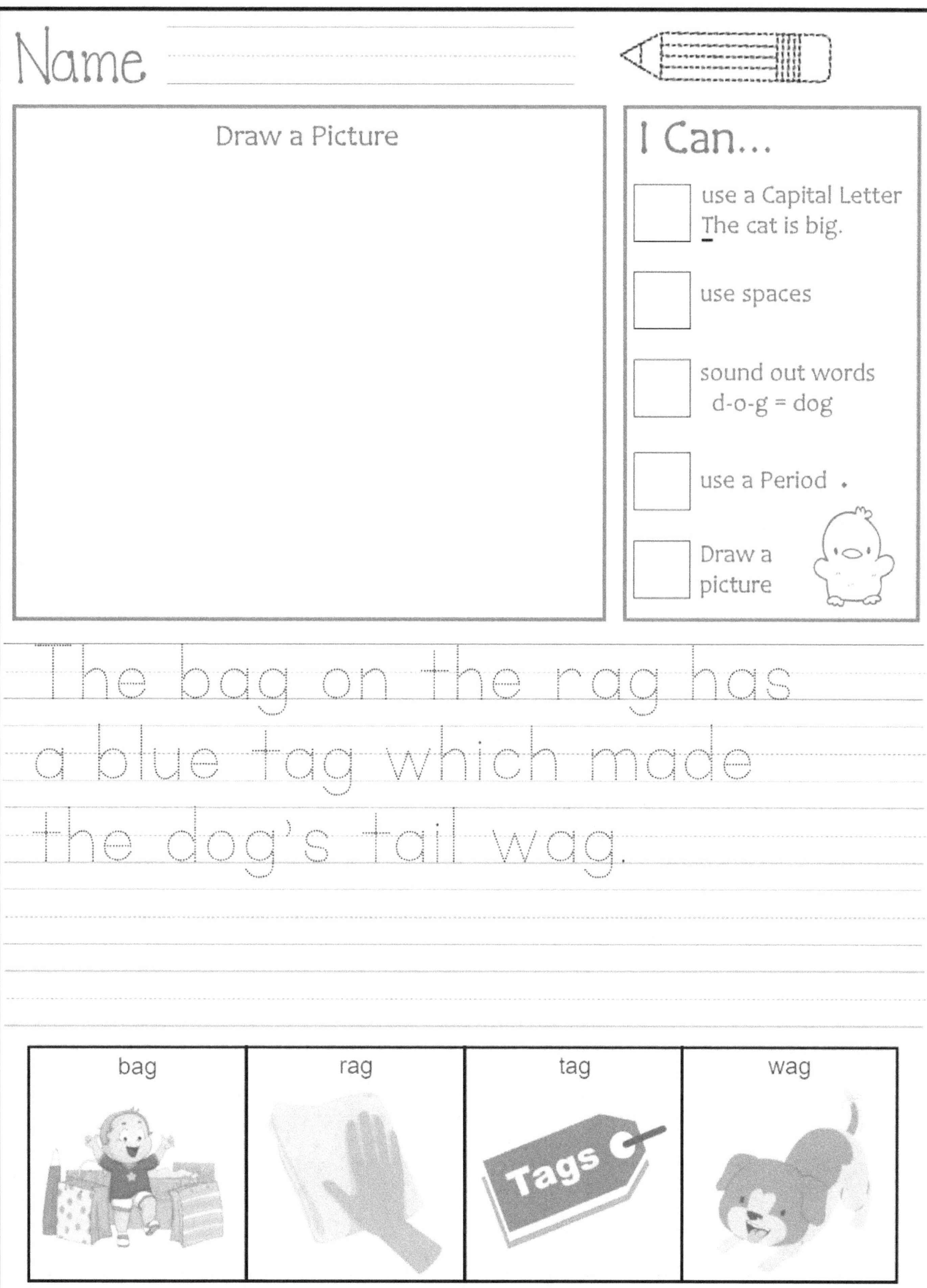

Name
Draw a Picture
I Can...
use a Capital Letter
The cat is big.
use spaces
sound out words
d-o-g = dog
use a Period .
Draw a picture
The bag on the rag has a blue tag which made the dog's tail wag.
bag
rag
tag
wag
Tags

Name: _________________ Date: _______

Today is: | Monday | Tuesday | Wednesday |
| Thursday | Friday |

Direction: Trace and read the sentences.

| can | man | pan | van |

I see a can of soda.

The man is happy.

The pan is dirty.

I see a big van.

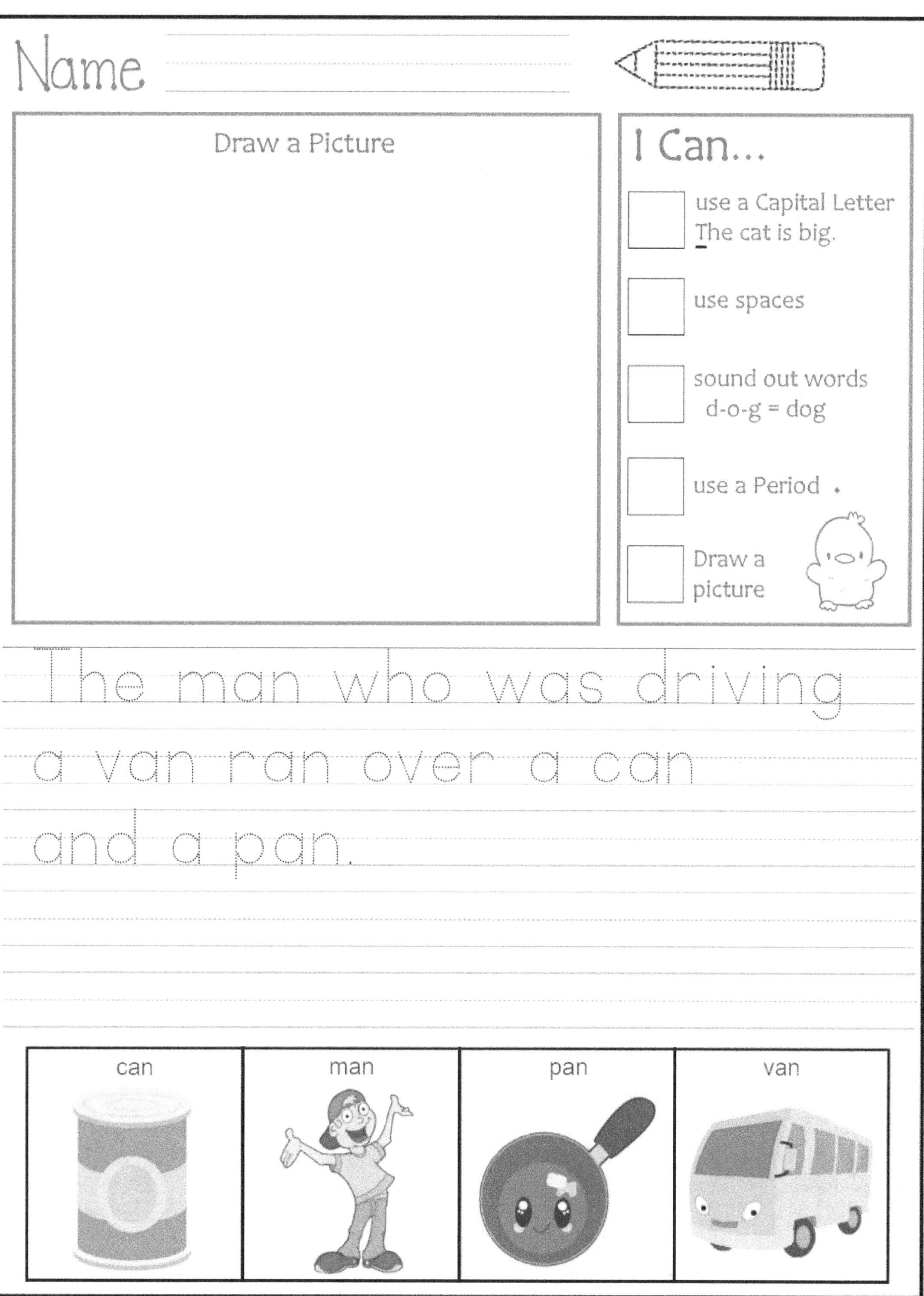

Name

Draw a Picture

I Can...

use a Capital Letter
The cat is big.

use spaces

sound out words
d-o-g = dog

use a Period .

Draw a
picture

The man who was driving
a van ran over a can
and a pan.

can

man

pan

van

Name: _______________ Date: _______________

Today is: [Monday] [Tuesday] [Wednesday] [Thursday] [Friday]

Direction: Trace and read the sentences.

| cut  | gut  | hut  | nut  |
|-----|-----|-----|-----|

He cut his nails.

He has a gut.

This is a small hut.

It is holding a nut.

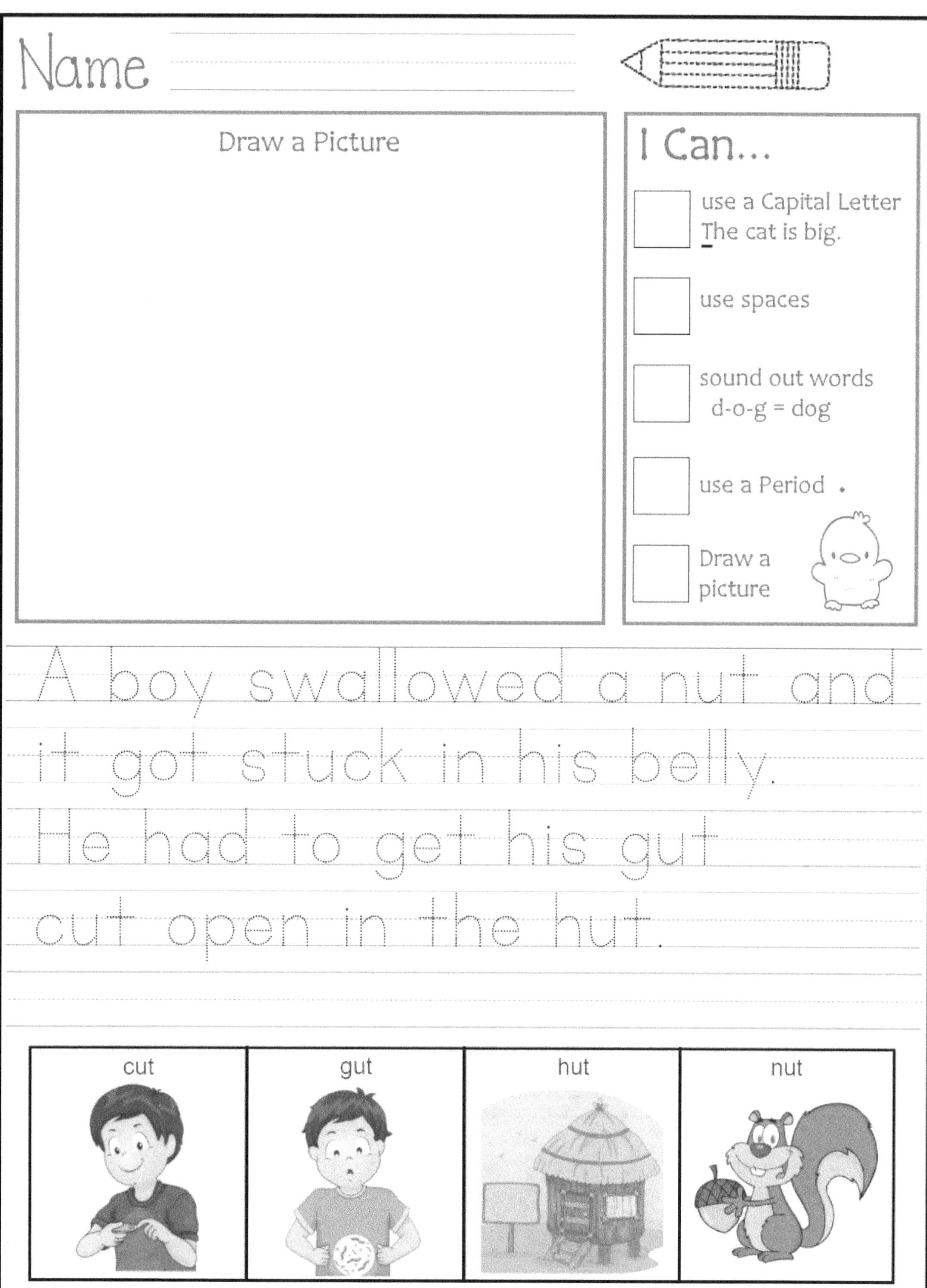


Name

Draw a Picture

I Can...
use a Capital Letter
The cat is big.

use spaces

sound out words
d-o-g = dog

use a Period .

Draw a
picture

A boy swallowed a nut and
it got stuck in his belly.
He had to get his gut
cut open in the hut.

cut
gut
hut
nut

Name: _______________ Date: _______________

Today is: [Monday] [Tuesday] [Wednesday]
[Thursday] [Friday]

Direction: Trace and read the sentences.

| fat  | cat  | hat  | mat  |
| --- | --- | --- | --- |

I see a fat dog.

This is my little cat.

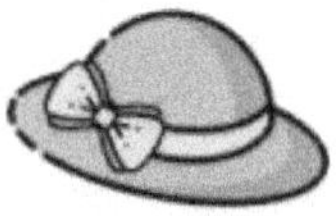

I like this hat.

I see a big mat.

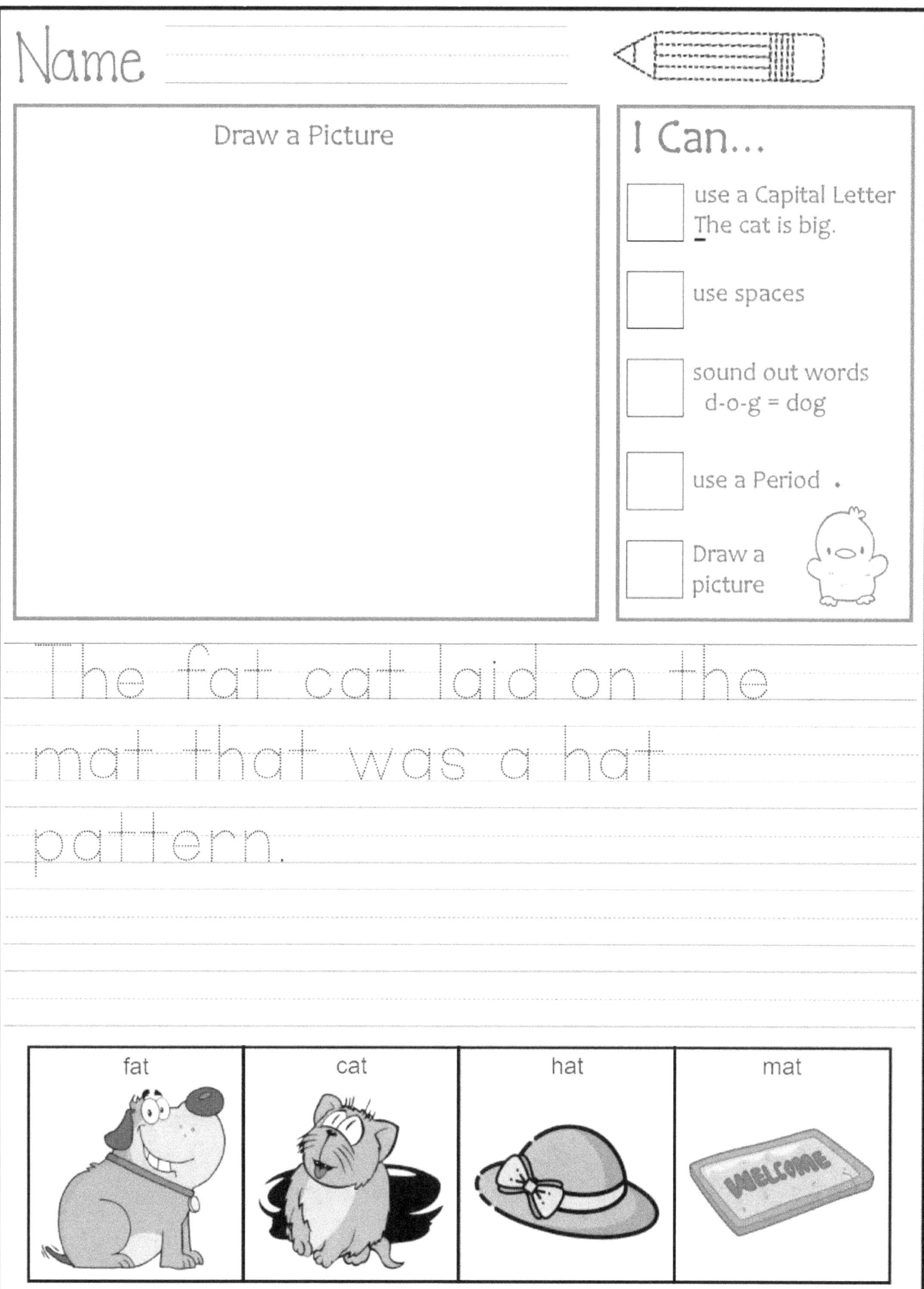

Name

Draw a Picture

## I Can...

- [ ] use a Capital Letter
  <u>T</u>he cat is big.

- [ ] use spaces

- [ ] sound out words
  d-o-g = dog

- [ ] use a Period .

- [ ] Draw a picture

The fat cat laid on the mat that was a hat pattern.

| fat | cat | hat | mat |
|-----|-----|-----|-----|

Name: _________________ Date: _______

Today is: Monday Tuesday Wednesday Thursday Friday

Direction: Trace and read the sentences.

| cab | lab | tab | crab |
|---|---|---|---|

The cab is fast.

The lab is exciting.

The tab is long.

We found a crab.

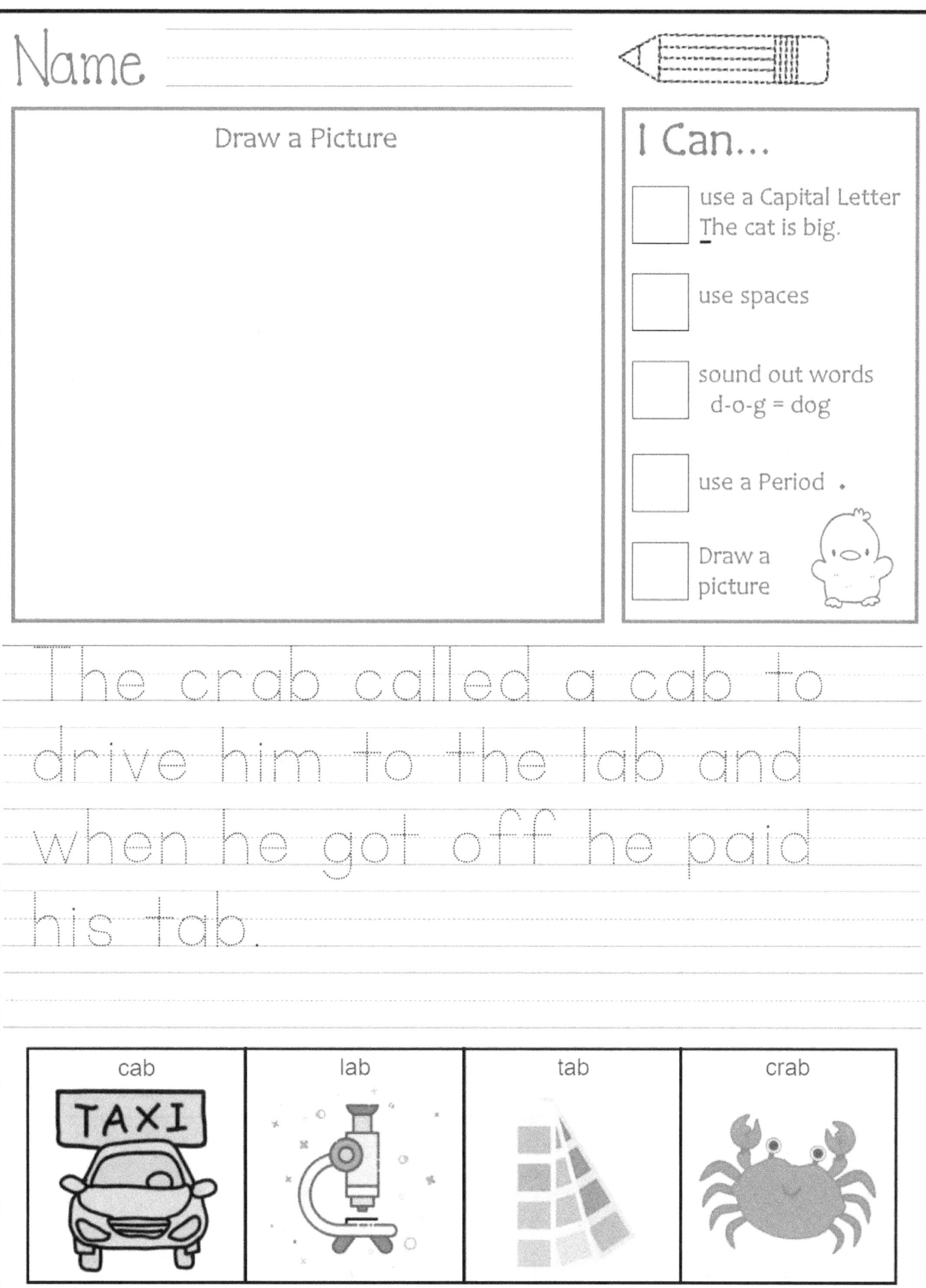

Name

Draw a Picture

## I Can...

- [ ] use a Capital Letter
  <u>T</u>he cat is big.
- [ ] use spaces
- [ ] sound out words
  d-o-g = dog
- [ ] use a Period .
- [ ] Draw a picture

The crab called a cab to drive him to the lab and when he got off he paid his tab.

| cab | lab | tab | crab |
|-----|-----|-----|------|

Name: _________________________ Date: _______________

Today is: [Monday] [Tuesday] [Wednesday] [Thursday] [Friday]

Direction: Trace and read the sentences.

| ham  | jam  | ram  | clam  |

I like to eat ham.

We like to eat jam.

The ram is big.

The clam is pretty.

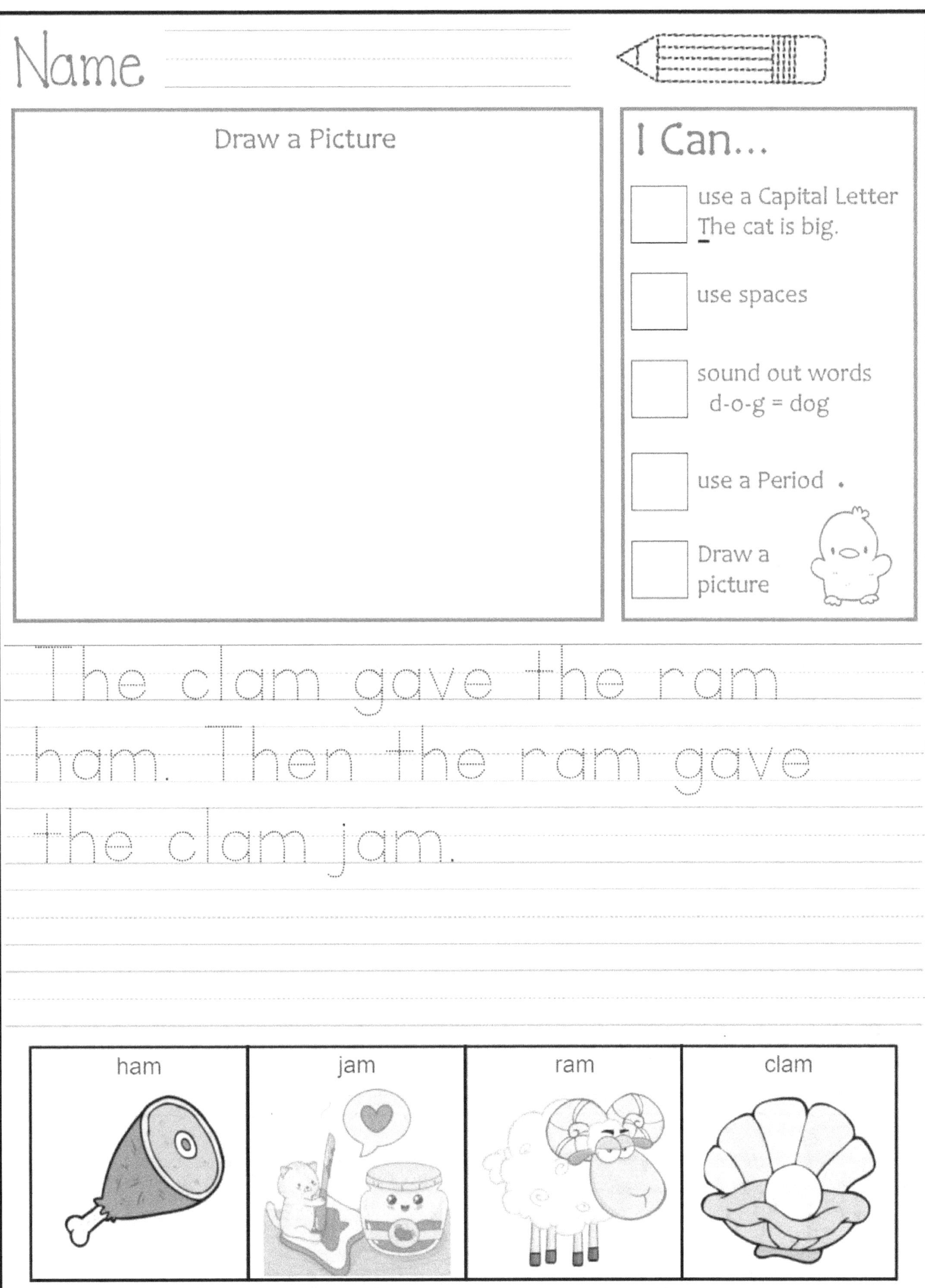


Name

Draw a Picture

I Can...

use a Capital Letter
The cat is big.

use spaces

sound out words
d-o-g = dog

use a Period .

Draw a
picture

The clam gave the ram
ham. Then the ram gave
the clam jam.

ham

jam

ram

clam

Name: _________________ Date: _____________

Today is: [ Monday ] [ Tuesday ] [ Wednesday ]
[ Thursday ] [ Friday ]

Direction: Trace and read the sentences.

| bed 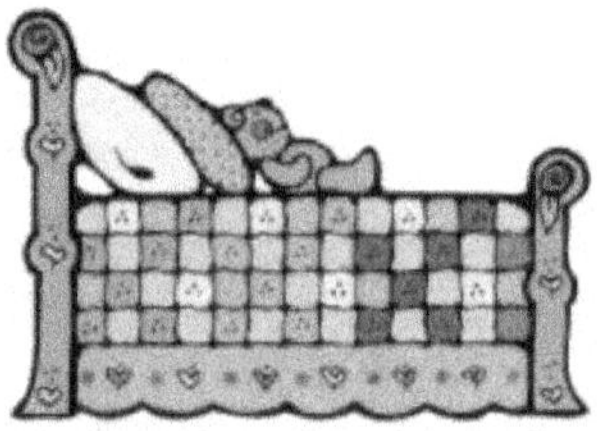 | led  | red  | wed  |
|---|---|---|---|

This is my little bed.

He led us to safety.

The apple is red.

He asks her to wed.

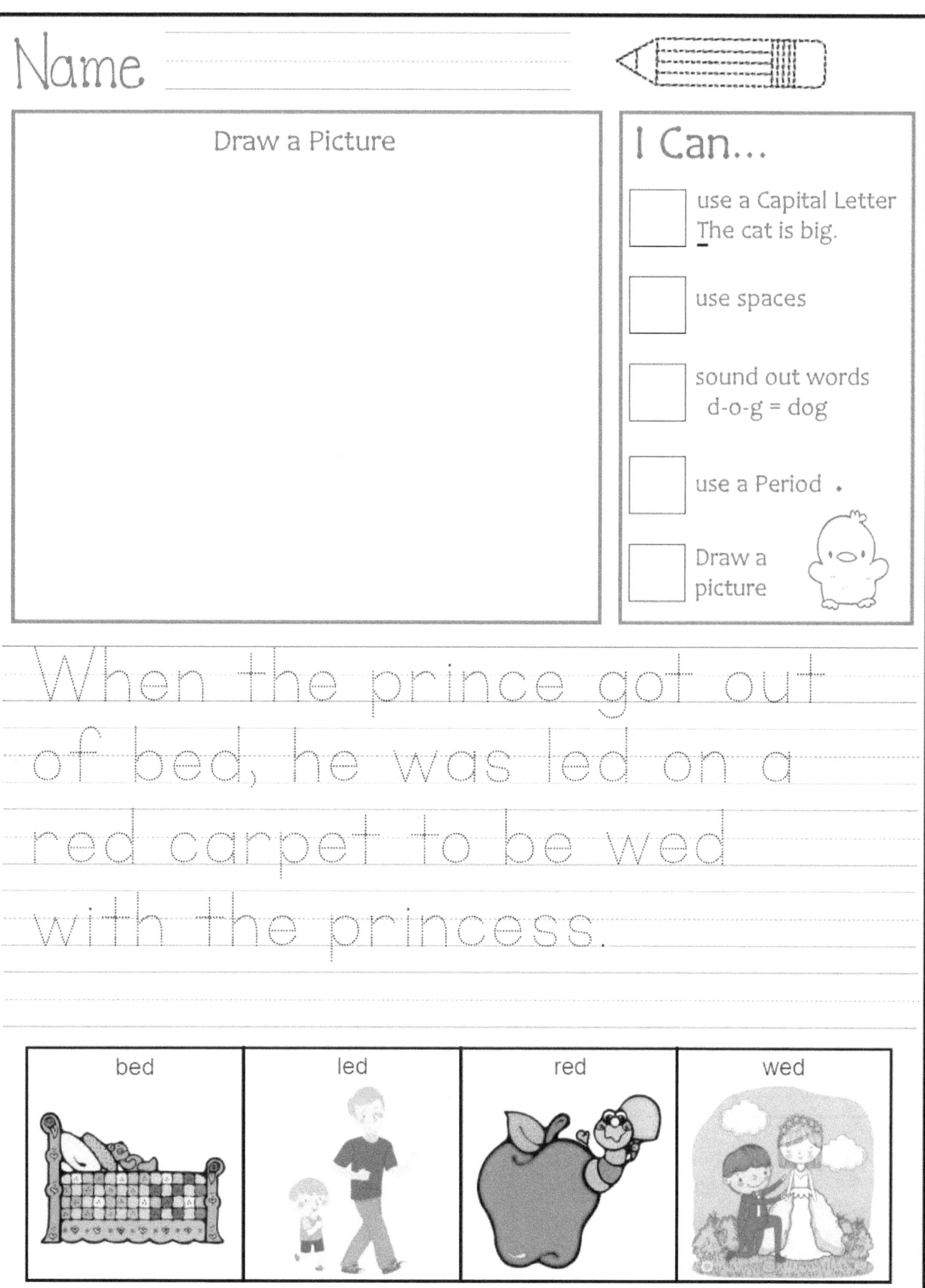


Name

Draw a Picture

I Can...

use a Capital Letter
The cat is big.

use spaces

sound out words
d-o-g = dog

use a Period .

Draw a
picture

When the prince got out
of bed, he was led on a
red carpet to be wed
with the princess.

bed
led
red
wed

Name: _________________ Date: _______________

Today is: [Monday] [Tuesday] [Wednesday]
[Thursday] [Friday]

Direction: Trace and read the sentences.

| bad | dad | mad | sad |
|-----|-----|-----|-----|

This apple is bad.

My dad is very kind.

The reindeer is mad.

The little cat is sad.

Name

Draw a Picture

## I Can...

- [ ] use a Capital Letter
  <u>T</u>he cat is big.

- [ ] use spaces

- [ ] sound out words
  d-o-g = dog

- [ ] use a Period .

- [ ] Draw a picture

I was bad so my dad got mad and now I am so sad.

| bad | dad | mad | sad |

Name: _________________ Date: _____________

Today is: [ Monday ] [ Tuesday ] [ Wednesday ]
[ Thursday ] [ Friday ]

Direction: Trace and read the sentences.

| den | hen | pen | ten |

It is a den.

The hens lay eggs.

She has a good pen.

The ten is smiling.

Name

Draw a Picture

I Can...

use a Capital Letter
The cat is big.

use spaces

sound out words
d-o-g = dog

use a Period .

Draw a
picture

The hen that lived in the
pen laid ten eggs
in her den.

den

hen

pen

ten

Name: __________________ Date: __________

Today is: Monday  Tuesday  Wednesday  Thursday  Friday

Direction: Trace and read the sentences.

| gum | mum | sum | drum |

I like to chew gum.

My mum is kind!

I can do a sum!

The drum is big.

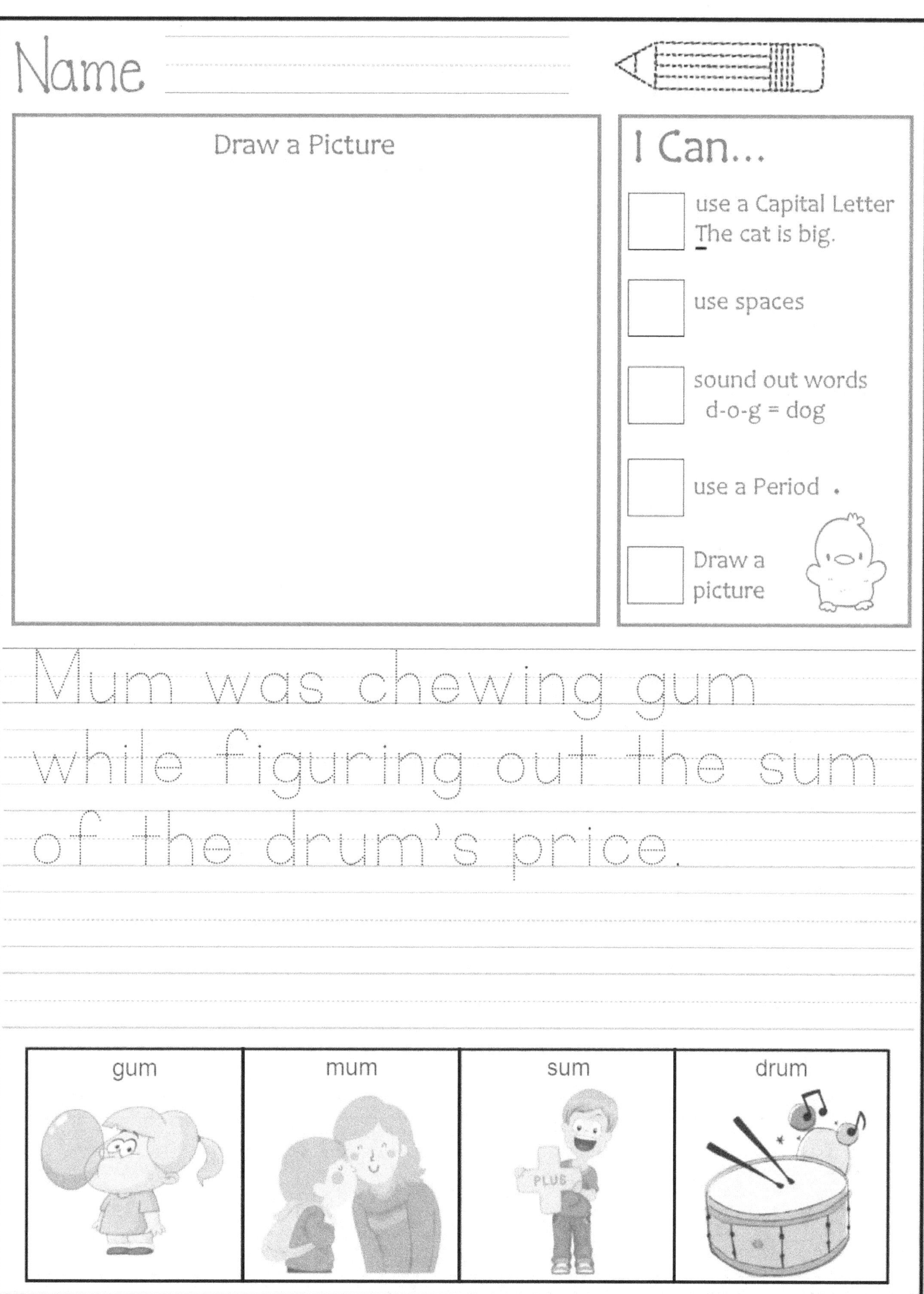

Name

Draw a Picture

I Can...

use a Capital Letter
The cat is big.

use spaces

sound out words
d-o-g = dog

use a Period .

Draw a
picture

Mum was chewing gum
while figuring out the sum
of the drum's price.

gum

mum

sum

drum

Name: _____________________  Date: _____________

Today is: | Monday | Tuesday | Wednesday |
| Thursday | Friday |

Direction: Trace and read the sentences.

| **bid**  | **hid**  | **kid**  | **lid** 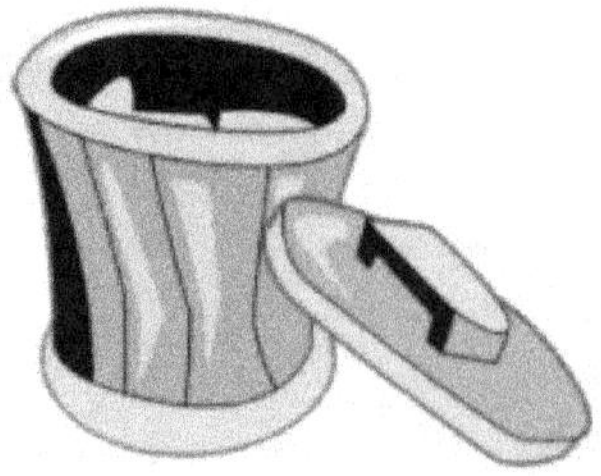 |

He likes to bid.

He is hiding.

The kid like to play.

I see a lid.

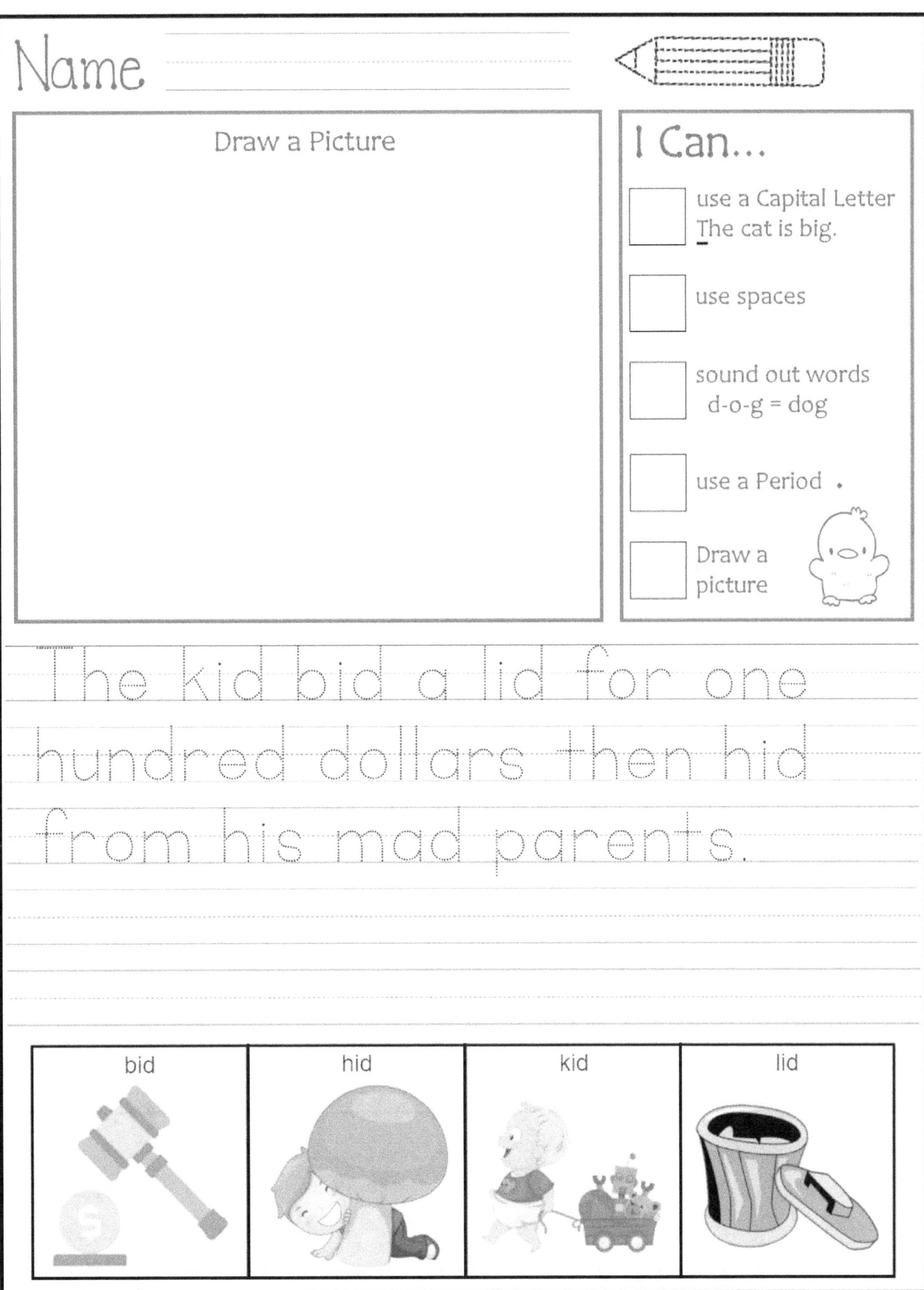

Name

Draw a Picture

I Can...

use a Capital Letter
The cat is big.

use spaces

sound out words
d-o-g = dog

use a Period .

Draw a
picture

The kid bid a lid for one
hundred dollars then hid
from his mad parents.

bid
hid
kid
lid

Name: ________________ Date: ____________

Today is: [Monday] [Tuesday] [Wednesday] [Thursday] [Friday]

Direction: Trace and read the sentences.

| big | dig | pig | wig |
|-----|-----|-----|-----|

That is a big pencil.

He will dig up a hole.

The pig is fat.

She puts on a wig.

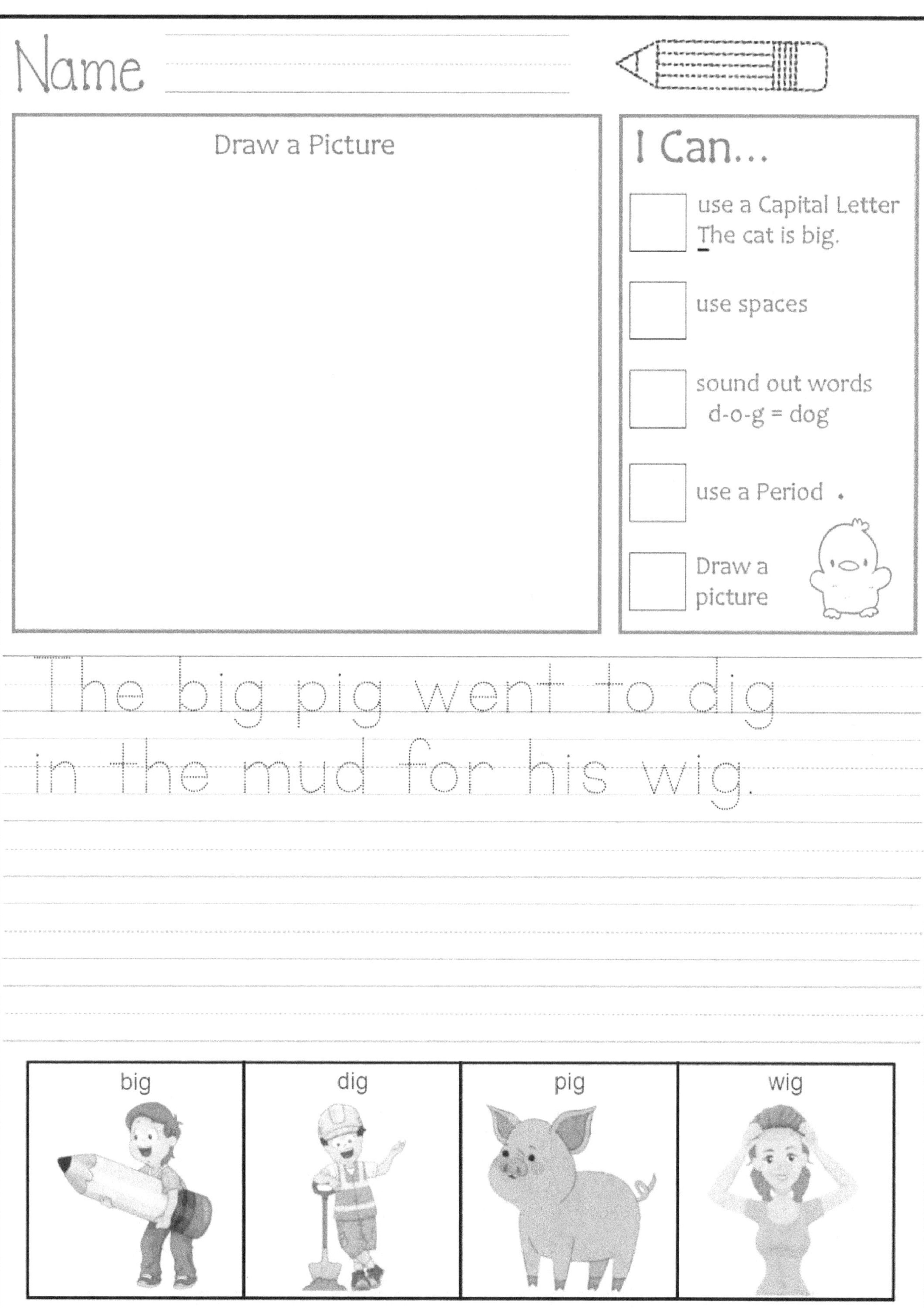


Name

Draw a Picture

I Can...

use a Capital Letter
The cat is big.

use spaces

sound out words
d-o-g = dog

use a Period .

Draw a
picture

The big pig went to dig
in the mud for his wig.

big

dig

pig

wig

Name: ___________________ Date: _______________

Today is: [Monday] [Tuesday] [Wednesday]
[Thursday] [Friday]

Direction: Trace and read the sentences.

| bin | fin | pin | win |
|---|---|---|---|

It is a recycle bin.

The shark has a fin.

The pin is pointy.

He won the match.

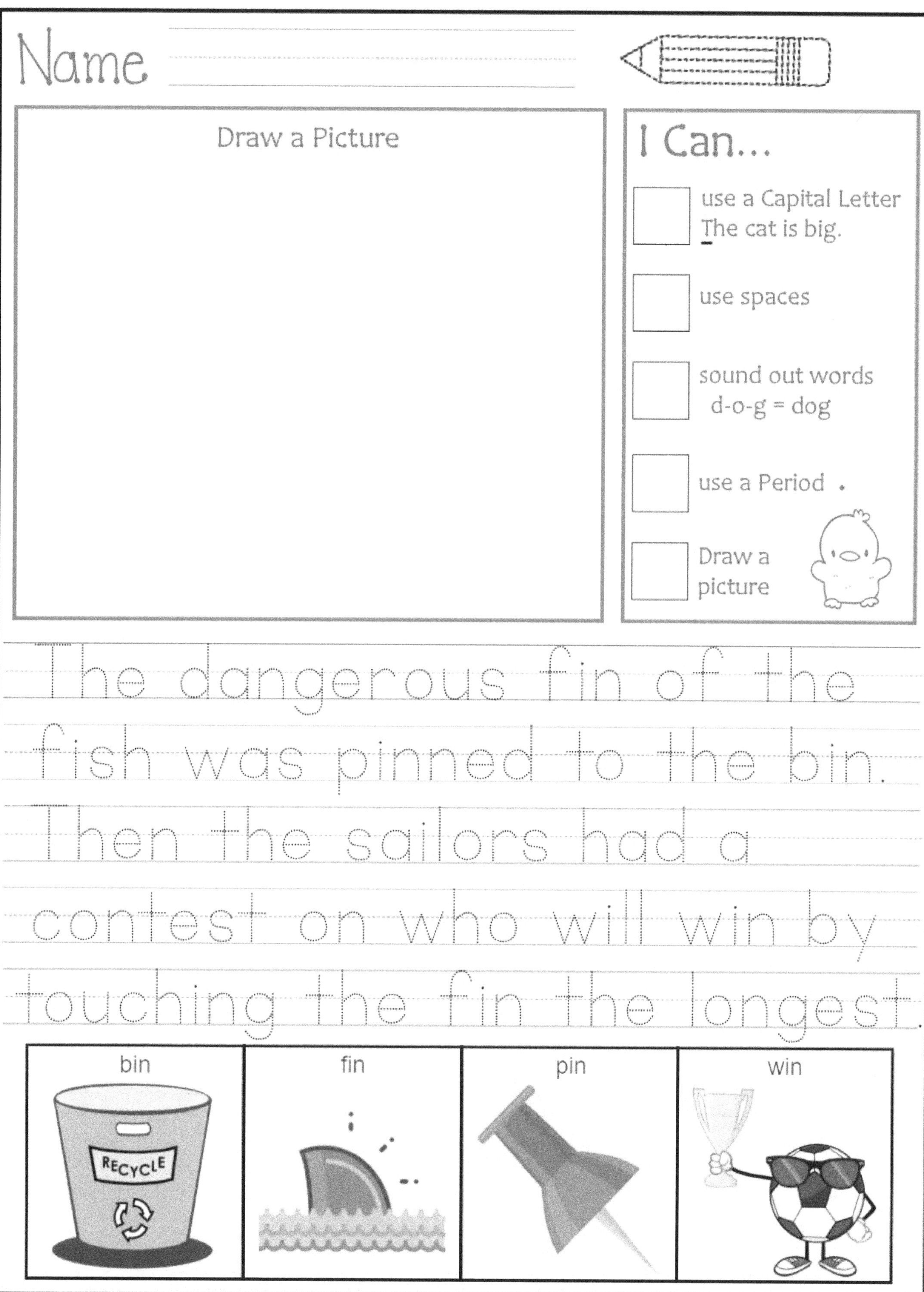

Name

Draw a Picture

I Can...

use a Capital Letter
The cat is big.

use spaces

sound out words
d-o-g = dog

use a Period .

Draw a
picture

The dangerous fin of the
fish was pinned to the bin.
Then the sailors had a
contest on who will win by
touching the fin the longest.

bin

fin

pin

win

RECYCLE

Name: _______________ Date: _______________

Today is: Monday | Tuesday | Wednesday | Thursday | Friday

Direction: Trace and read the sentences.

| hip  | lip  | nip  | sip  |
|---|---|---|---|

This is my hip.

Her lips are red.

It is nipping its toy.

She is sipping.

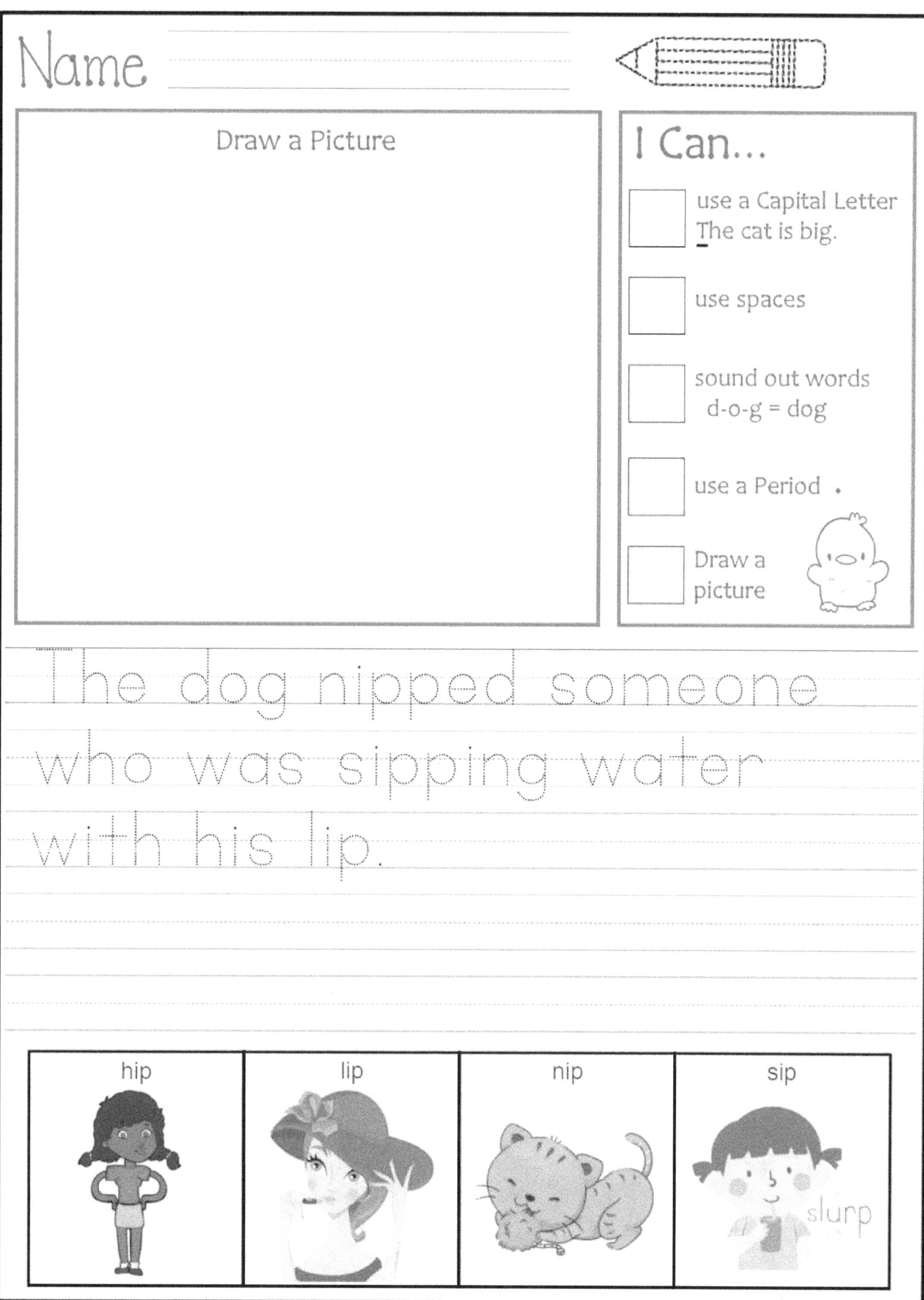

Name

Draw a Picture

I Can...

use a Capital Letter
The cat is big.

use spaces

sound out words
d-o-g = dog

use a Period .

Draw a
picture

The dog nipped someone
who was sipping water
with his lip.

hip
lip
nip
sip
slurp

Today is: Monday  Tuesday  Wednesday  Thursday  Friday

Direction: Trace and read the sentences.

| fit | hit | kit | sit |
|-----|-----|-----|-----|

It is perfectly fit.

They hit each other.

That is a safety kit.

He is sitting.

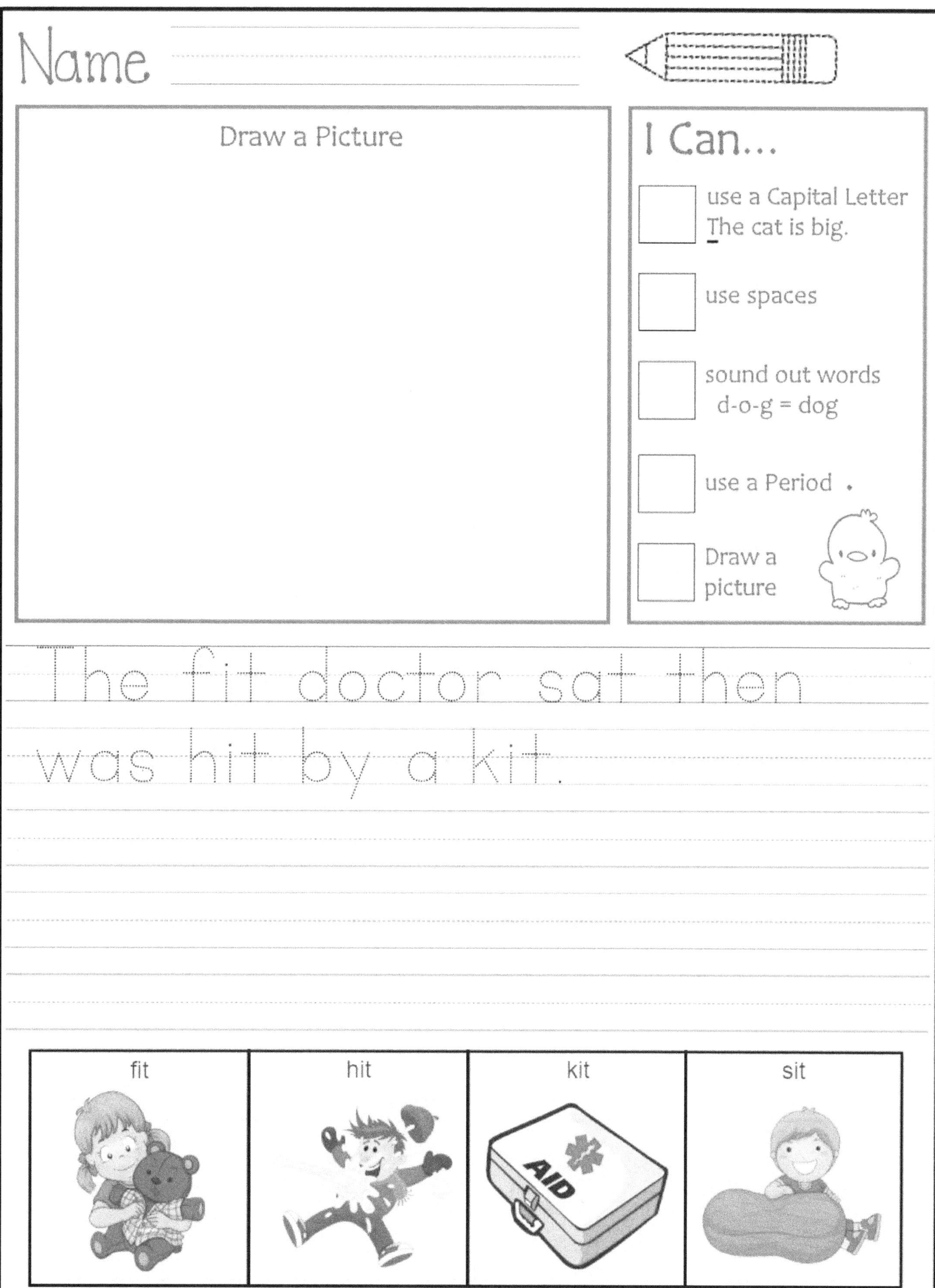


Name

Draw a Picture

I Can...

use a Capital Letter
The cat is big.

use spaces

sound out words
d-o-g = dog

use a Period .

Draw a
picture

The fit doctor sat then
was hit by a kit.

fit

hit

kit

sit

AID

Name: _______________ Date: _______________

Today is: Monday | Tuesday | Wednesday | Thursday | Friday

Direction: Trace and read the sentences.

| cob  | job  | rob  | sob  |
| --- | --- | --- | --- |

I ate corn on the cob

This is my job.

He is robbing.

The girl is sobbing.

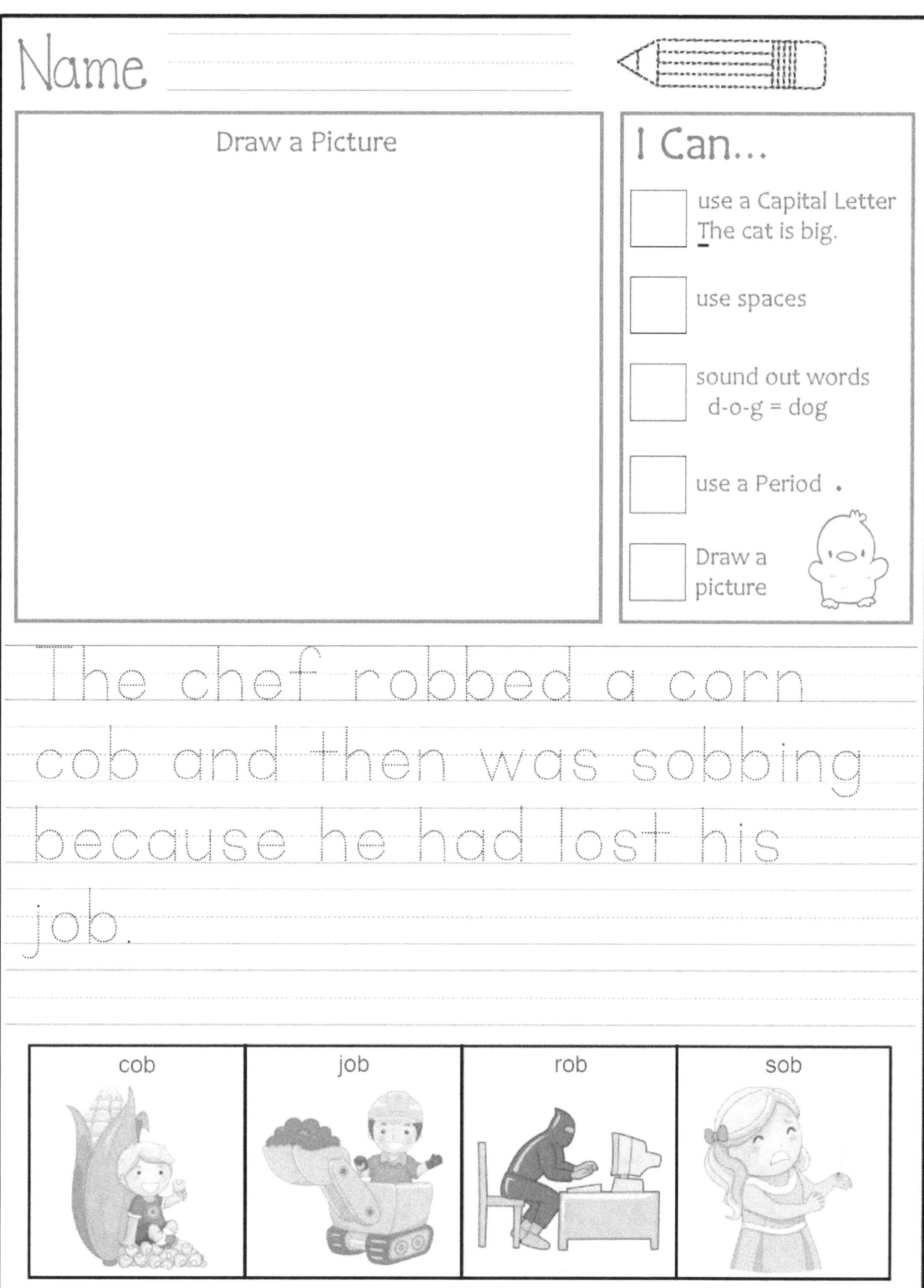

Name

Draw a Picture

I Can...

use a Capital Letter
The cat is big.

use spaces

sound out words
d-o-g = dog

use a Period .

Draw a
picture

The chef robbed a corn
cob and then was sobbing
because he had lost his
job.

cob
job
rob
sob

Name: ___________________ Date: ______________

Today is: Monday   Tuesday   Wednesday

Thursday   Friday

Direction: Trace and read the sentences.

| dog  | hog  | jog  | log 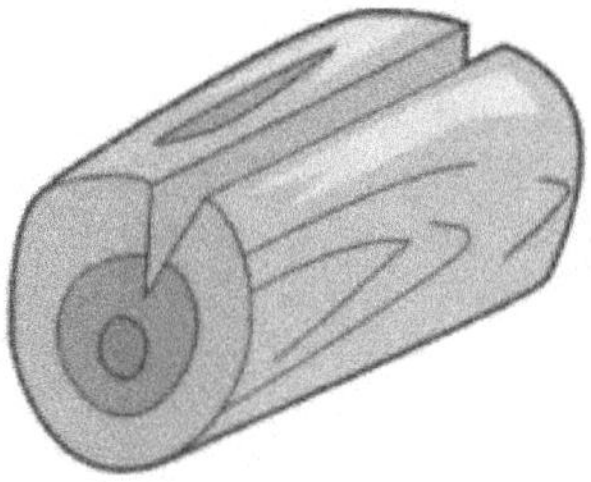 |

The dog is thrilled.

The hog is big.

She is jogging.

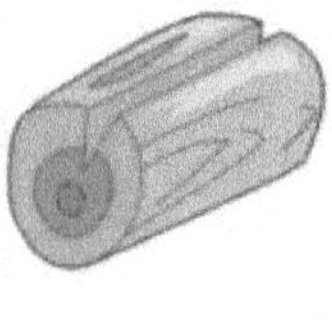

The log is small.

Name

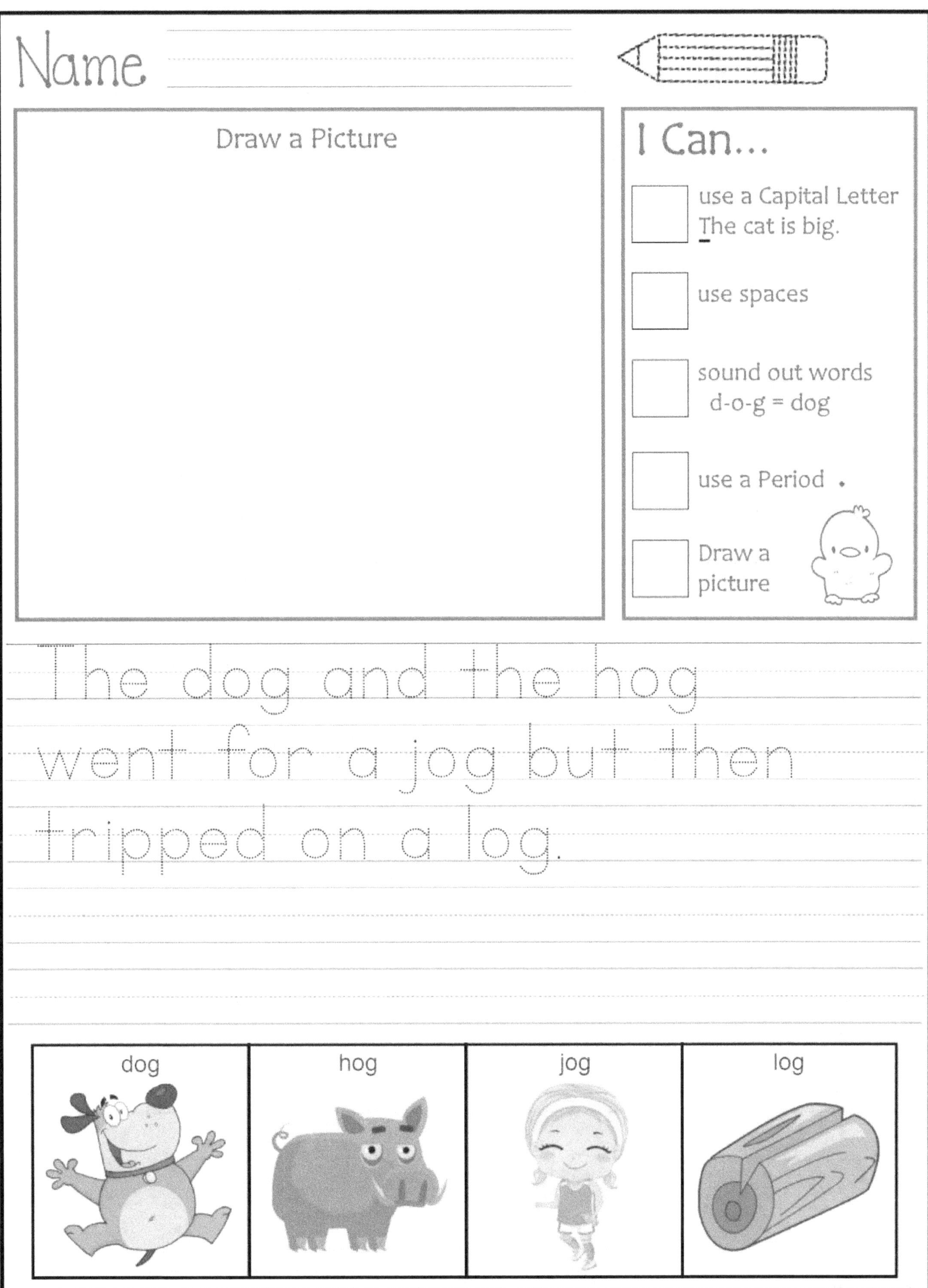
Draw a Picture

I Can...
use a Capital Letter
The cat is big.

use spaces

sound out words
d-o-g = dog

use a Period .

Draw a
picture

The dog and the hog
went for a jog but then
tripped on a log.

dog
hog
jog
log

Name: _______________ Date: _______

Today is: Monday | Tuesday | Wednesday | Thursday | Friday

Direction: Trace and read the sentences.

| bug 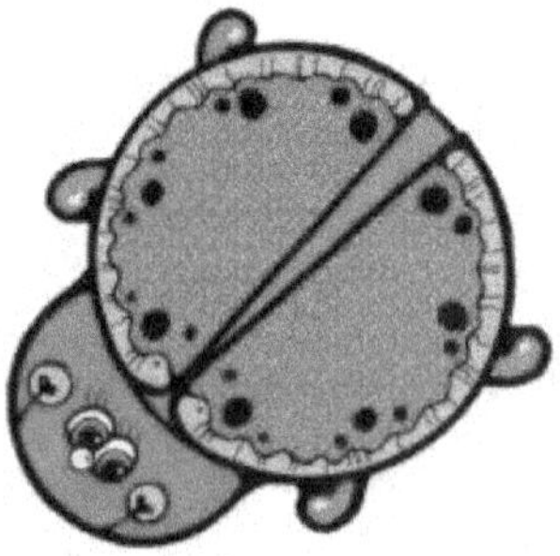 | hug  | jug  | mug  |

The bug is colorful.

She is hugging.

The jug has milk in it.

He has a mug.

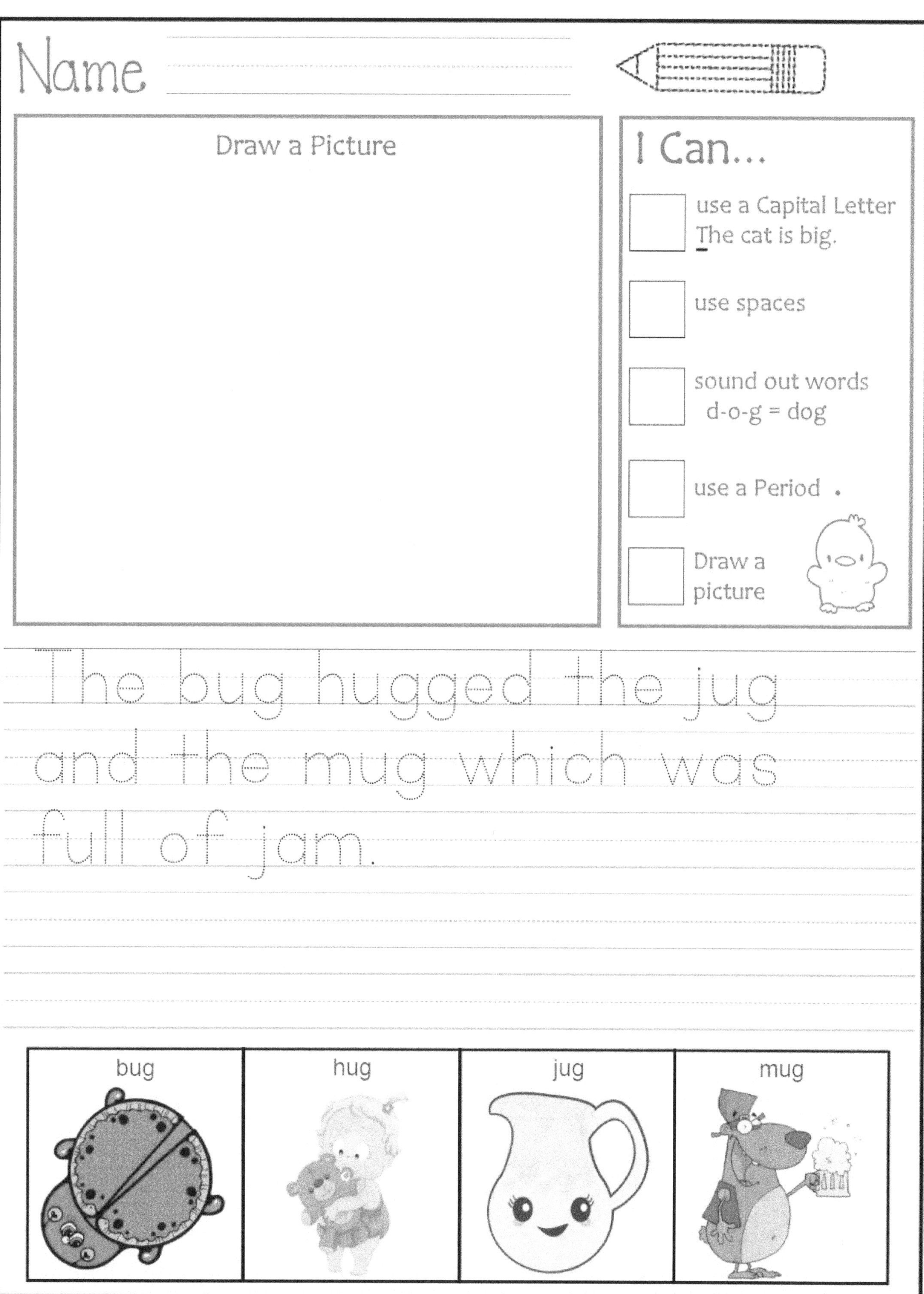


Name

Draw a Picture

I Can...

use a Capital Letter
The cat is big.

use spaces

sound out words
d-o-g = dog

use a Period .

Draw a
picture

The bug hugged the jug
and the mug which was
full of jam.

bug
hug
jug
mug

Name: _______________ Date: _______________

Today is: [Monday] [Tuesday] [Wednesday]
[Thursday] [Friday]

Direction: Trace and read the sentences.

| cot | dot | hot | pot |
|-----|-----|-----|-----|

This is my cot.

There are many dots.

It is very hot.

He has a plant pot.

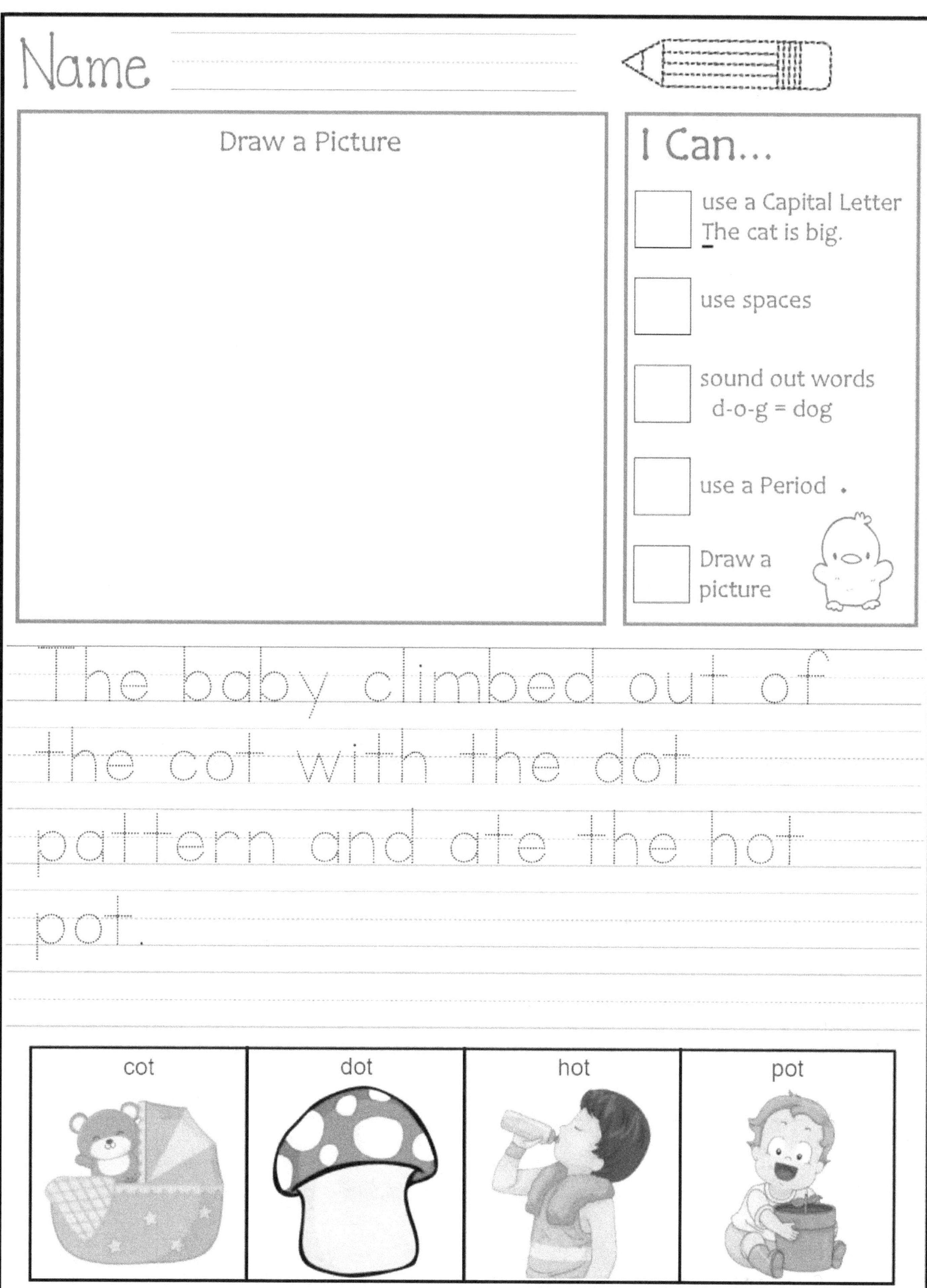

Name
Draw a Picture
I Can...
use a Capital Letter
The cat is big.
use spaces
sound out words
d-o-g = dog
use a Period .
Draw a picture
The baby climbed out of the cot with the dot pattern and ate the hot pot.
cot
dot
hot
pot

Name: _______________  Date: _______________

Today is: Monday  Tuesday  Wednesday
Thursday  Friday

Direction: Read the words and make a sentence.

| fun | gun | run | sun |
|-----|-----|-----|-----|

Draw a Picture

## I Can...

- [ ] use a Capital Letter
  The cat is big.
- [ ] use spaces
- [ ] sound out words
  d-o-g = dog
- [ ] use a Period  .
- [ ] Draw a picture

Name: _______________________  Date: _______________

Today is: Monday | Tuesday | Wednesday
          Thursday | Friday

Name: _________________________ Date: _____________

Today is: [ Monday ] [ Tuesday ] [ Wednesday ]
[ Thursday ] [ Friday ]

Direction: Read the words and make a sentence.

| bag | rag | tag | wag |
|-----|-----|-----|-----|

Name

Draw a Picture

## I Can...

☐ use a Capital Letter
The cat is big.

☐ use spaces

☐ sound out words
d-o-g = dog

☐ use a Period .

☐ Draw a picture

Name: ___________________ Date: ___________________

Today is: Monday Tuesday Wednesday
Thursday Friday

Name: _________________________ Date: _______________

Today is: Monday  Tuesday  Wednesday

Thursday  Friday

Direction: Read the words and make a sentence.

| can | man | pan | van |
| --- | --- | --- | --- |

Name

Draw a Picture

I Can...

use a Capital Letter
The cat is big.

use spaces

sound out words
d-o-g = dog

use a Period .

Draw a
picture

Name: _________________ Date: _________________

Today is:  Monday   Tuesday   Wednesday

Thursday   Friday

Name: _______________________ Date: _______________________

Today is: Monday   Tuesday   Wednesday

Thursday   Friday

Direction: Read the words and make a sentence.

| cut | gut | hut | nut |
|-----|-----|-----|-----|

Name

Draw a Picture

## I Can...

☐ use a Capital Letter
<u>T</u>he cat is big.

☐ use spaces

☐ sound out words
d-o-g = dog

☐ use a Period .

☐ Draw a picture

Name: _______________    Date: _______________

Today is: Monday  Tuesday  Wednesday  Thursday  Friday

Name: _______________________  Date: _______________________

Today is: | Monday | Tuesday | Wednesday |
| Thursday | Friday |

Direction: Read the words and make a sentence.

| fat | cat | hat | mat |

Name

Draw a Picture

## I Can...

- [ ] use a Capital Letter
  The cat is big.

- [ ] use spaces

- [ ] sound out words
  d-o-g = dog

- [ ] use a Period  .

- [ ] Draw a
  picture

Name: _________________ Date: _________________

Today is: Monday | Tuesday | Wednesday | Thursday | Friday

Name: ________________________  Date: ____________

Today is:  Monday   Tuesday   Wednesday

Thursday   Friday

Direction: Read the words and make a sentence.

| cab | lab | tab | crab |
|-----|-----|-----|------|

Name ______________

Draw a Picture

## I Can...

- [ ] use a Capital Letter
  <u>T</u>he cat is big.

- [ ] use spaces

- [ ] sound out words
  d-o-g = dog

- [ ] use a Period .

- [ ] Draw a
  picture

Name: _______________ Date: _______________

Today is: Monday Tuesday Wednesday Thursday Friday

Name: _________________________ Date: _________________

Today is: | Monday | Tuesday | Wednesday |
Thursday | Friday |

Direction: Read the words and make a sentence.

| ham | jam | ram | clam |

<br>

ham ______________________________

jam ______________________________

ram ______________________________

clam ______________________________

Name _______________________

Draw a Picture

## I Can...

- ☐ use a Capital Letter
  The cat is big.

- ☐ use spaces

- ☐ sound out words
  d-o-g = dog

- ☐ use a Period .

- ☐ Draw a picture

Name: _________________ Date: _________________

Today is:  Monday  Tuesday  Wednesday  Thursday  Friday

Name: ______________________  Date: ______________

Today is:  Monday   Tuesday   Wednesday

Thursday   Friday

Direction: Read the words and make a sentence.

| bed | led | red | wed |
|-----|-----|-----|-----|

Name

Draw a Picture

## I Can...

- [ ] use a Capital Letter
  <u>T</u>he cat is big.

- [ ] use spaces

- [ ] sound out words
  d-o-g = dog

- [ ] use a Period .

- [ ] Draw a picture

Name: _______________________  Date: _______________________

Today is: Monday | Tuesday | Wednesday | Thursday | Friday

Name: _________________ Date: _______________

Today is: [Monday] [Tuesday] [Wednesday]
[Thursday] [Friday]

Direction: Read the words and make a sentence.

| bad | dad | mad | sad |
| --- | --- | --- | --- |

Name

Draw a Picture

Name: _______________________ Date: _______________

Today is: [Monday] [Tuesday] [Wednesday] [Thursday] [Friday]

Name: _________________________  Date: _____________

Today is:  Monday  Tuesday  Wednesday
           Thursday  Friday

Direction: Read the words and make a sentence.

| den | hen | pen | ten |
|-----|-----|-----|-----|

_______________________________

_______________________________

_______________________________

_______________________________

Name ________________

<table>
<tr><td>Draw a Picture</td><td>I Can...</td></tr>
</table>

## Draw a Picture

## I Can...

- ☐ use a Capital Letter
  <u>T</u>he cat is big.

- ☐ use spaces

- ☐ sound out words
  d-o-g = dog

- ☐ use a Period .

- ☐ Draw a picture

Name: _______________________   Date: _________

Today is: Monday   Tuesday   Wednesday   Thursday   Friday

Name: _______________  Date: _______________

Today is: Monday  Tuesday  Wednesday  Thursday  Friday

Direction: Read the words and make a sentence.

gum     mum     sum     drum

Name

Draw a Picture

## I Can...

- [ ] use a Capital Letter
  The cat is big.

- [ ] use spaces

- [ ] sound out words
  d-o-g = dog

- [ ] use a Period .

- [ ] Draw a picture

Name: _______________________  Date: _______________

Today is:  Monday   Tuesday   Wednesday
           Thursday   Friday

Name: ___________________ Date: ___________

Today is: Monday | Tuesday | Wednesday | Thursday | Friday

Direction: Read the words and make a sentence.

| bid | hid | kid | lid |
| --- | --- | --- | --- |

Name

Draw a Picture

## I Can...

- [ ] use a Capital Letter
  The cat is big.

- [ ] use spaces

- [ ] sound out words
  d-o-g = dog

- [ ] use a Period .

- [ ] Draw a picture

Name: _______________   Date: _______________

Today is: | Monday | Tuesday | Wednesday |
| Thursday | Friday |

Name: ___________________ Date: ___________________

Today is: Monday  Tuesday  Wednesday  Thursday  Friday

Direction: Read the words and make a sentence.

| big | dig | pig | wig |
|-----|-----|-----|-----|

Name

Draw a Picture

## I Can...

- [ ] use a Capital Letter
  <u>T</u>he cat is big.

- [ ] use spaces

- [ ] sound out words
  d-o-g = dog

- [ ] use a Period  .

- [ ] Draw a picture

Name: _______________________  Date: _______________

Today is: [Monday] [Tuesday] [Wednesday]
[Thursday] [Friday]

Name: _______________________  Date: _______________

Today is:  [ Monday ]  [ Tuesday ]  [ Wednesday ]
           [ Thursday ]  [ Friday ]

Direction: Read the words and make a sentence.

| bin | fin | pin | win |
|-----|-----|-----|-----|

Name

Draw a Picture

## I Can...

- [ ] use a Capital Letter
  <u>T</u>he cat is big.

- [ ] use spaces

- [ ] sound out words
  d-o-g = dog

- [ ] use a Period .

- [ ] Draw a picture

Name: _______________________    Date: _______________

Today is: Monday | Tuesday | Wednesday | Thursday | Friday

Name: _________________________  Date: _________________________

Today is: [Monday] [Tuesday] [Wednesday]
[Thursday] [Friday]

Direction: Read the words and make a sentence.

| hip | lip | nip | sip |

Name

Draw a Picture

## I Can...

- [ ] use a Capital Letter
  The cat is big.

- [ ] use spaces

- [ ] sound out words
  d-o-g = dog

- [ ] use a Period .

- [ ] Draw a picture

Name: _________________ Date: _________

Today is: [Monday] [Tuesday] [Wednesday]
[Thursday] [Friday]

Today is: Monday | Tuesday | Wednesday | Thursday | Friday

Direction: Read the words and make a sentence.

| fit | hit | kit | sit |
|-----|-----|-----|-----|

Name

Draw a Picture

## I Can...

- [ ] use a Capital Letter
  <u>T</u>he cat is big.

- [ ] use spaces

- [ ] sound out words
  d-o-g = dog

- [ ] use a Period .

- [ ] Draw a picture

Name: _______________________ Date: _______________

Today is: Monday | Tuesday | Wednesday

Thursday | Friday

Name: _________________ Date: _______________

Today is: [Monday] [Tuesday] [Wednesday]
[Thursday] [Friday]

Direction: Read the words and make a sentence.

| cob | job | rob | sob |
|-----|-----|-----|-----|

Name _______________________

## Draw a Picture

## I Can...

- [ ] use a Capital Letter
  <u>T</u>he cat is big.

- [ ] use spaces

- [ ] sound out words
  d-o-g = dog

- [ ] use a Period .

- [ ] Draw a picture

Name: ___________________  Date: ___________

Today is: Monday  Tuesday  Wednesday  Thursday  Friday

Name: _________________________  Date: _______________

Today is:  Monday   Tuesday   Wednesday

Thursday   Friday

Direction: Read the words and make a sentence.

| dog | hog | jog | log |
| --- | --- | --- | --- |

Name

Draw a Picture

## I Can...

- [ ] use a Capital Letter
  <u>T</u>he cat is big.

- [ ] use spaces

- [ ] sound out words
  d-o-g = dog

- [ ] use a Period .

- [ ] Draw a picture

Name: _______________________     Date: _______________

Today is: Monday  Tuesday  Wednesday  Thursday  Friday

Name: _________________ Date: _______________

Today is: | Monday | Tuesday | Wednesday |
| Thursday | Friday |

Direction: Read the words and make a sentence.

| bug | hug | jug | mug |

Name

Draw a Picture

## I Can...

- [ ] use a Capital Letter
  The cat is big.

- [ ] use spaces

- [ ] sound out words
  d-o-g = dog

- [ ] use a Period  .

- [ ] Draw a
  picture

Name: _______________________     Date: _______________

Today is: [ Monday ] [ Tuesday ] [ Wednesday ]
[ Thursday ] [ Friday ]

Name: _________________________ Date: _________________

Today is: [Monday] [Tuesday] [Wednesday]
[Thursday] [Friday]

Direction: Read the words and make a sentence.

| cot | dot | hot | pot |
|-----|-----|-----|-----|

Name

Draw a Picture

## I Can...

☐ use a Capital Letter
The cat is big.

☐ use spaces

☐ sound out words
d-o-g = dog

☐ use a Period .

☐ Draw a picture

Name: ___________________  Date: ___________

Today is: | Monday | Tuesday | Wednesday | Thursday | Friday |

www.ingramcontent.com/pod-product-compliance
Lightning Source LLC
Chambersburg PA
CBHW081352160726
48000CB00010B/3305